Bibi Dumon Tak is the author of *Soldier Bear* and *Mikis and the Donkey* (both Eerdmans), both of which won the Mildred L. Batchelder Award. In 2018 Bibi received the Theo Thijssen Prize, the highest honor for children's authors in the Netherlands. She has previously collaborated with Annemarie van Haeringen on *Scout's Heaven* (Eerdmans). The original edition of *Leave a Message in the Sand* was shortlisted for the Jan Wolkers Prize for the best Dutch nature book.

Annemarie van Haeringen is the illustrator of *Scout's Heaven* (Eerdmans), *Coco and the Little Black Dress* (NorthSouth), *How to Knit a Monster* (Clarion), and *Mr. Matisse and His Cutouts* (NorthSouth). She is a three-time winner of the Gouden Penseel Award, given to the year's best illustrated book in the Netherlands, and has also received the award's silver honor. Visit Annemarie's website at www.annemarievanhaeringen.nl.

Laura Watkinson translates books for children and adults from Dutch, Italian, and German. She was the translator for Bibi Dumon Tak's Batchelder-winning books *Soldier Bear* and *Mikis and the Donkey*, and she also worked with Bibi Dumon Tak and Annemarie van Haeringen on their book *Scout's Heaven*. Visit Laura's website at www.laurawatkinson.com.

First published in the United States in 2020
by Eerdmans Books for Young Readers,
an imprint of Wm. B. Eerdmans Publishing Co.
Grand Rapids, Michigan

www.eerdmans.com/youngreaders

Text copyright © 2018 by Bibi Dumon Tak
Illustrations copyright © 2018 by Annemarie van Haeringen
Original title: *Laat een boodschap achter in het zand*
First published in 2018 by Em. Querido's Uitgeverij, Amsterdam
English language translation copyright © Laura Watkinson, 2020

Manufactured in China.

28 27 26 25 24 23 22 21 20   1 2 3 4 5 6 7 8 9

ISBN 978-0-8028-5548-0

A catalog record of this book is available from the Library of Congress.

Illustrations created with ink and watercolor.

Written by Bibi Dumon Tak

Illustrated by Annemarie van Haeringen

Translated by Laura Watkinson

Leave a Message in the Sand

Poems about Giraffes, Bongos,
and Other Creatures with Hooves

Eerdmans Books for Young Readers

Grand Rapids, Michigan

The Giraffe

Hey there, you walking watchtower
with your long-necked superpower!
You can see your way above the crowds.
But what's it like so near the clouds?
Don't you feel cold all the way up there?
Can you even breathe the air?
Does the rain blow wet and the wind blow dry?
Do you bump your head upon the sky?
Do you ever trip and fall?
Don't you ever get tired at all?
How does the blood reach your brain?
Hey, and is the rainbow full of rain?

The giraffe has a heart
as strong as a slingshot.
A powerful pump—
thud, thump, thud, thump.
With every beat,
the blood shoots around,
making an impressive sound,
whooshing and gushing and raging and roaring,
up through that endless neck and up and up,
through thick, thick veins,
to power the giraffe's distant brains.

Hey, Giraffe,
that heart of yours,
that hellish hammer,
that drives the blood up into your head,
could we borrow it for a moment?
And your neck too?
To see if what people say is true,
that rain begins up there as snow
before it falls down here below.

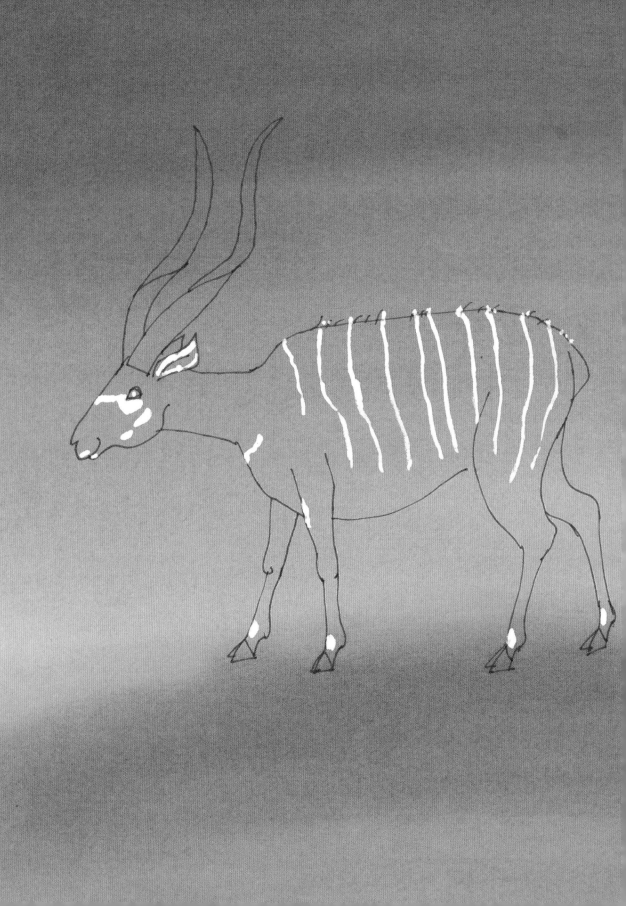

The Bongo

Put your phone on silent,
no talking now,
no moving allowed,
shhh!
Who's that tiptoeing timidly
through the night?
It's the African bongo, shining bright,
an animal with flashlights on its cheeks,
an animal with gold paint on its coat.

What's it doing out in the open
with its ears as big as sails?
What's it doing in plain sight?
Even its ribs are giving off light.

Why is it standing there, stamping away,
stomping its hooves on the wet clay,
does it think no one's watching,
waiting, stalking?
No hyenas, pythons,
cheetahs out hunting?
What's that it's doing?
What's it licking and chewing?
Hey, be careful!
Danger! Stop!

Risking its own life,
the bongo ventures out of
the jungle every night.
To hunt for salt and sand and mud,
and pieces of burnt wood,
for sodium, magnesium,
copper, calcium, and zinc.
It eats all the minerals in sight
to make itself glow bongo bright
cheeks and ribs and hooves and skin
or else its bongo lights go dim.
Clean white coat growing crusty.
Shiny gleam turning dull and dusty.

So, Bongo,
quickly lick your lights back on
and trot into the jungle,
to shine and glow among the green,
hidden away, somewhere unseen,
in a nice, snug spot that's safe for prey,
where you can put on your own
private light display.

The Wild Boar and the Pig

Hey, porky!

Hi, cuz, haven't heard from you in a while. What have you been up to?

You know, just rooting around.

Nice.

Yup. How about you, baldy?

The usual. Life behind bars. ☺

Hey, I met a guy yesterday.

You didn't!

I did!

And?

He was covered in blood.

Huh? Blood? Who? What? Why?

It's fall, you know?

Fall? What's that again?

It's when the nuts fall out of the trees.

Yeah, right. I only know one nut.

Huh?

The farmer.

Oh yes, that guy of yours. But yeah, this guy of mine, he'd been fighting for me—and he won!

Oh, so he's a tough guy, huh? Cool!

Sure is. Had this big slash right across his chest. But you should have seen the other guy. Knocked out in the bushes. Such a boring boar!

Whew! Sometimes I'm happy to be safe inside, cuz.

And he's got tusks the size of antlers!

Tusks? Antlers? I have no idea what they are, but I'll take your word for it.

You should get out more, cuz. The nuts are good this year. In fact, I'd better go eat some more. Nice talking to you. Oh, and say hi to the piglets. How many was it this time?

Fifteen of them left now. It was more. All pink and wriggling and newly born.

Awww. I'm hoping for seven. In March.

I'll have my trotters crossed for you. Be careful out there in that scary forest, cuz!

Sure will! Stay tame, okay? And keep that curl in your tail! 🖤

The Cape Buffalo

In partnership with our sponsors

Are you tired of a life without fear?
And do you want that to change?
Then you've come to the right team!
Of all the animals on the savannah,
we're the ones who'll make you scream!

WHEN WE'RE AROUND
DANGER IS GUARANTEED

CAPE BUFFALO TOURS!

We're unguided missiles
that can shoot off in any direction,
and we have more horsepower than you can handle.

Our foreheads are plated with horns
made of armored keratin.
Our bull bars can silently
toss you through the air.
We are the tanks of Africa.
Unpredictable.
Impulsive.
And we travel in platoons.
And sometimes squads.
And now and then just one angry male.

Want an adventure?
Then book a trip to meet our herd head on.
We'll add some fire to your life.
And if you book right now
we'll give you a second attack for free!

At CB Tours, we make memories you won't forget.
We guarantee you'll never feel safe again,
because the fear of buffaloes
is a fear that lasts a lifetime.

Why not try our new line?
The CBXL50—
an extra-large-caliber
Cape buffalo.
To ensure lasting panic.
Only available from CB!
What a rush!

The Mountain Goat

Call the police!
Call the fire crew!
Quick! Dial 9-1-1!
Or 1-1-2!
And let's hope we're not too late,
because spring has just begun!
We have to save them!
Emergency services, safety nets, sirens, alarm!
Make sure no one comes to harm!
Because the mountain goat is heading off again
across crumbling rocks and glaciers and ice,
climbing to the highest height.
Is she trying to give us a fright?
Is she going to pierce the sun?
To touch the stars with her horns?
What's she doing up there with that big belly?!
Does she mean to turn our knees to jelly?
Waaaaaahhh! Waaaaaahhh! That siren sound
says: Climb up there and bring her down!
Now!

A mountain goat mother has her baby
not in a cave or in a bush,
but on the edge of a ravine,
at the top of a rocky wall—
because gravel, granite,
and sharp stones
are her best friends of all.
Every year, their rock-hard hands,
so solid and many centuries old,
welcome baby goats into the fold.

Humans raise a hue and cry.
It's an emergency! Now! No, don't ask why!
It's code red!
While down into the valley, no goat dares,
as there are prowling wolves, lynxes, pumas, and bears.
That's no place for a little goat kid,
so you can see why Mommy Goat did what she did.
Mountain goat mothers climb to spots
where the wind ripples on every side,
a curtain of ice blown from far and wide.
But it's a place where their young can be safe.
So turn off the flashing lights and sirens.
Stand down and set the code to green.
The world is still turning.
Let those mountain goat moms
have a nice and cozy place to stay
in their mountain hideaway.
They just need a little time and space
to give birth in their own cold, high, safe place.

The Lesser Mouse-Deer

Why don't we see more of you?
Well, you're tiny!
Only 12 inches tall,
18 inches long,
and 4.5 pounds in weight.
The smallest hooved animal on Earth.
Likes to live alone.
Address: southeast Asia, around the equator.
Says the webpage.
That's everything about you,
lesser mouse-deer:
a big blank page
with a tiny photo—and that's all.
So do you know what?
Why don't we take a closer look?

The Lesser Mouse-Deer
(a second attempt)

On hooves the size of fingertips.
With eyes like little chocolate chips,
tripping on matchstick legs through the trees
almost blown away by the slightest breeze.
Spindly
skittish
lesser creature,
so lonely in the big wild woods.
Lonely? Really? Lesser? Huh?

The female nearly always
has a baby in her belly.
Once it's born,
she goes out
and makes a new baby right away.
Three baby showers every year.
A baby by your side,
a baby in your belly,
and your friends nearby?
Do you call that lonely?
I don't think so, webpage.
But is the lesser mouse-deer bothered?
No. Because the lesser mouse-deer
is perfectly sure
that lesser really does mean more.
Hey, internet, stop the hate.
When you're a mouse-deer,
lesser is great!

The Warthog

Big lump of clay,
all brown and gray,
gross pool of mud,
with sludge for blood,
made up of bristles,
skin soft as thistles.
Which dirty hole
did you come crawling out of?

Have you ever taken a look at yourself?
With your hair all clumps
and your face all bumps?
With your tusks sticking out
of that brown, wrinkly snout?
With your diet made of gloop
and rhinoceros poop?

Dear readers,
we present to you
the monstrous warthog!
Look! Just one sight
is such a fright!
Hey, Warty,
what are you even doing here?
Get off our planet!
Find somewhere else to live!

Somewhere else to live?
Wait a minute, the warthog has so much to give!
          Huh? Why's that?
Well, it feeds half of Africa.
          But how?
With itself.
          With itself?
That's right.

The warthog would barely hurt a fly,
but the whole savannah is after that guy.
   That's so mean!
Exactly! Cool it a bit, everyone.
If anyone's nasty about the warthog,
we'll personally, um . . .

. . . feed them to the lions!

The Dik-Dik and the Hippopotamus

Live on Radio Impala from Pretoria, South Africa

Welcome to the studio, Hippopotamus! Great to have you here. And may I say it's a huge . . .
What? What? What's that you said?
What do you mean by "huge"?

Um . . . Just that it's a huge pleasure to finally speak with you.
We've been wanting to interview you for a long time. And I'm sure the wait will . . .
The weight? What's that about my weight?
No, no, I'm sure the long wait will have been worthwhile.
Oh, I see. Then why didn't you say so?
I don't like insults, you know.

Insults? No, we'd never dare!
You know, hippos don't put up with nonsense.
If we don't like the look of you,
we'll make sure you know about it.
It doesn't matter who you are.
We. Will. Fight. You.
We're not as cute and cuddly as we seem.
We know how to fight, how to bash,
how to bite, and how to smash.

And, um, would you like to tell our listeners a bit more about that?
It's quite simple. We bite our enemies in two.
Call it aggressive if you like,
but it's what we do.
And we never forgive insults.

Not even when the insult was an accident?
Accident? There's no such thing.
Hippopotamuses hate "by accident."
Oh, and we also hate "on purpose."

But imagine that . . .
Imagine . . . another disgusting word.
We'll crush it and crunch it, mash it and munch it.
Sickening.
Nauseating.
Stomach-turning.
Vomit-churning.
So, Dik-Dik,
let's get to the point.

Well, um, could it be that . . .
Could? Could?!
Another awful word.
Disgusting! Repulsive! Revolting!
Do you really want to die,
you tiny little radio guy?
Any more of this and . . .

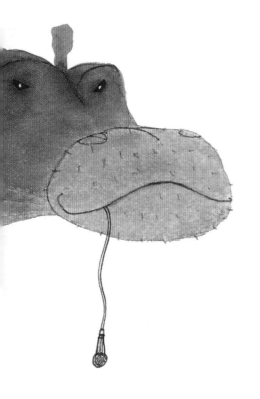

But maybe . . .
Maybe?!
How dare you?!
Maybe is . . .
repugnant.
Repellent.
Deeply disgusting.
It's hardly surprising
my anger is rising.
You fake antelope!
You hollow-horned dope!
Think you can interview me?
You're a loser! So sue me!
Radio? Who put that idea into your head?
You should've stayed home in your dry riverbed.

I'm sorry, Hippopotamus, but could you please
put down the microphone?
I'm following the law of the jungle.
Eat or be eaten! Munch!

But, please, just listen . . .
Crack! Crunch!

That sound, dear listeners, at home and on the road,
was just the microphone snapping. No need to worry.

Munch!
Eek!
Crack!
Eeeek!
Crunch!
Eeeeeek!

Hmm. So puny, pitiful, pathetic.
And such a titchy, tiny, teensy vocabulary.
Maybe he should have used a dik-dik-diktionary!

The Arabian Oryx

First there were lots
then a few
and then none.
The wild oryx died out.
Not because of drought
or thirst
or the scorching sun.
Not because of the storms of sand mixed with stones.
Or the fog, the heat, the sudden cold.
No, it was a constant hail of bullets
that made the oryx disappear.

Okay, that's enough.
Just stop! Bring on the next animal.
We can't take any more.
Give us another dik-dik or a dromedary.
We don't need to know everything,
just because it's true.
Goodbye, Oryx,
it was nice meeting you,
or not, whatever,
all the best,
farewell.

Wait a moment!
We're not done yet!
They hadn't actually all died out.
Someone went and caught the last few.
And then they took them to a zoo.
        Really?
Yes!
Introduced them to the last oryxes in cages,
And then waited and waited and waited for ages.
Until . . . Yes! Some calves were born.
        And then? And then?

They made those tame guys wild again.
It took a few years and then a few more,
but you know good things are worth waiting for.

      And now? And now?
The Arabian oryx made history,
having child after child.
And was the first (nearly) extinct animal
to be returned to the wild.

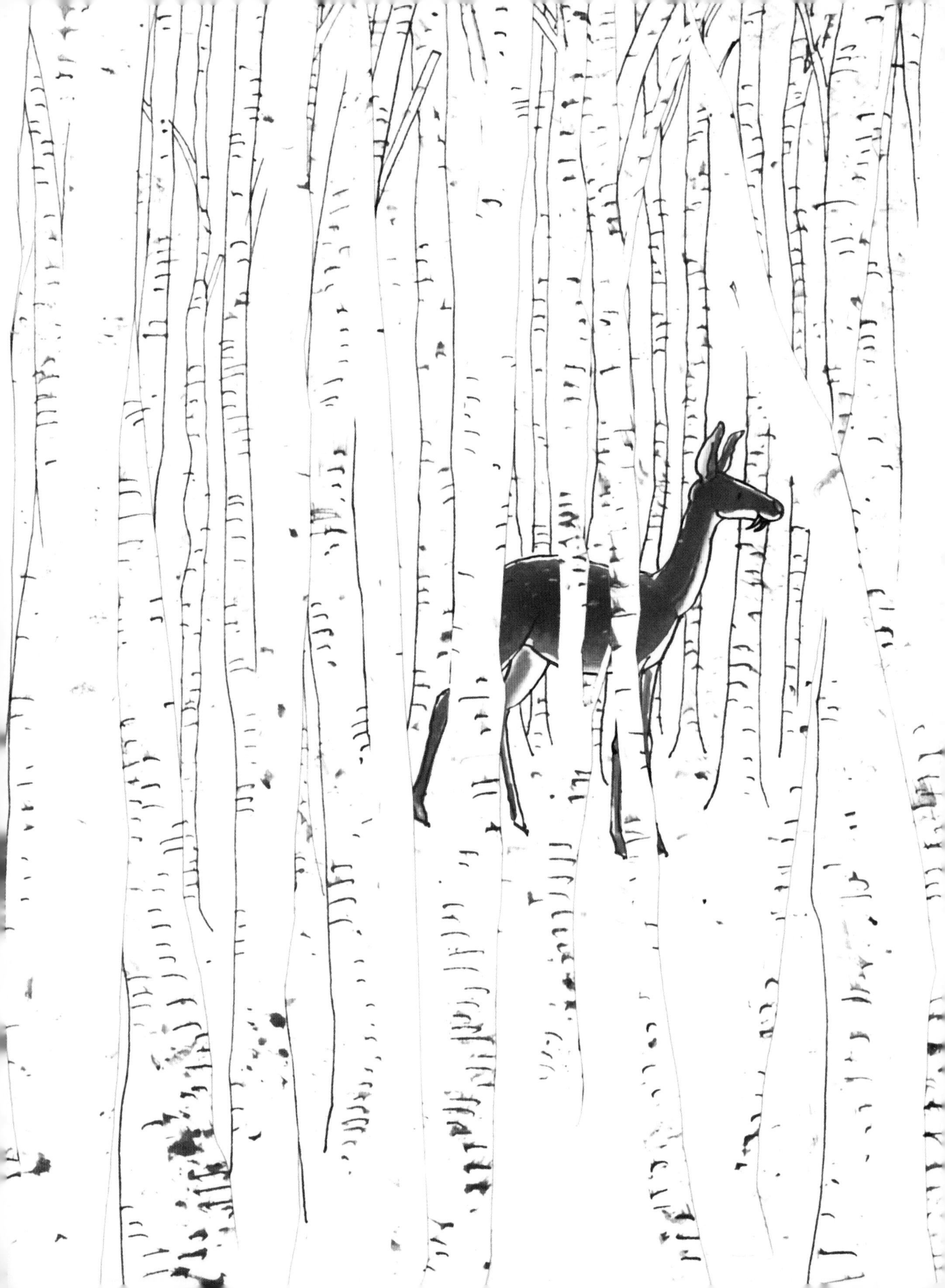

The Siberian Musk Deer

When the night
turns off the light,
and darkness
fills the skies,
that's when the musk deer wakes
and blinks its sleepy eyes.

Flames flashing
along its throat,
starlight splashing
over its coat,
this little deer roams the taiga.
Is it cute?
Yes, pretty cute,
with its two little vampire fangs.

Vampire fangs? What are they for?
To kill other deer?
To fill them with fear?
To give them a scare?
To bite and to tear?
No, no, no.
To fight for the ladies.
But it's not just about strength.
There's something else as well:
the male deer's powerful, musky smell!

The musk stags wander the pitch-dark land,
their weapons always close at hand,
while the ladies' nostrils twitch
feeling a most irresistible itch
to sniff up the scent of soil, of moss and mud,
of leaf and bark and sleeping bud,
the smell of the day when it is done,
a beating wing, the setting sun,
a hint of pee,
a hint of poo,
the spring grass beaded with evening dew,
the breeze through a sultry birch-tree wood,
it's a perfume that does a doe such good.
Pure musk straight from the gland
of the smelliest male deer in the land.

And while those macho men
flash their fangs,
the ladies all around them say:
Guys, just put your weapons away.
Not interested! Nope!
What do we really want?
What do you think?
Always and forever,
your delicious, manly stink!

The Vicuña

Where space begins,
at the end of the sky,
where the plateau floats,
high and dry,
where the stars rule at night
and clouds shelter from the wind,
that's where the vicuña lives.
On lonely heights
with air that is far too thin,
not a great place if you have to breathe,
that's where you'll find the vicuña,
happily inhaling the empty air,
because it has magic in its blood.

As humans lie panting,
breath nearly gone,
oxygen masks on,
the vicuña makes another sprint
because its blood is so strong,
so full of life,
like soda popping with bubbles,
fizzing all the way
up into its head.

When our blood
is kind of dead
and a little less red,
the vicuña's cells live on.
It breathes the thin air up there—
and it's one of the very few—
from the high plateau of Bolivia
to the Altiplano of Peru.

Hey, Vicuña,
next time you dash across the heavens,
could you stop for a moment
to pass on a message, if you would?
Because someone we love
has gone there for good.

The Wild Bactrian Camel

Male seeks female(s).
Male camel, single. Wild.
6yo. From Mongolia, Gobi Desert.
Kids no prob.
Strong. V. faithful.
Flexible. Can take the heat (+120 °F)
and extreme cold (-40 °F).
Willing to relocate.
Lady from Lop Nur welcome.
Or whole harem.
Not tame
(humans = lame).
R u the one(s)?
Then leave a message in the sand.
There are only a thousand of us now.
It's so quiet and empty here
and my ♥ is the loneliest in the land.

The White-Tailed Deer

Is the red carpet out?
Is the camera rolling?
Are the barriers in place?
Where are the microphones?
And how's the light?
Are all the spots positioned just right?
Drums and trumpets ready to play?
We have so many fans here today!
Yes! Here he comes,
the most famous animal on four hooves.
How about a big hand?
Let's give a huge cheer
to the world's most amazing
white-tailed deer!

Hey, little fawn, can we ask you something?
Just between us, dear,
and no one else needs to hear.
But almost a hundred years have gone by,
so don't you think it's time to grow up?
For antlers to grow on your head,
for your coat to fade to brown from red?
Shake off those white spots.
Wake up, little fawn,
you can wait another century,
but your mother still won't come back.

Yes, grow up, little fawn!
Leave the red carpet behind
and become a stag.
Time to trot away from Hollywood
and put an end to your movie career.
Find a herd,
win a wife,
and—this might sound mean—but
get a life!
Be big! Not small! Be a stag, not a fawn!
You know it's what your mom
would have said.
Even though she's long, long
dead.

The Okapi

Subject: all ungulates
Complaint: discrimination
Your email address: okapi@okapi.cd

Dear Editors,

There is something that,
as an even-toed ungulate,
as a relative of the giraffe,
as a compatriot of the bongo
from Congo,
I need to get off my chest.

We all walk on two toes,
or four, like the hippopotamus, which is fine,
but one toe more or one toe less—
is it really such a big deal?
Shouldn't odd-toed ungulates
be allowed in this book?
Where are the rhinoceros, the zebra, the tapir?
What I mean is: Look,
a hoof is a hoof is a hoof.
Equality for ungulates, both odd and even!

And that is why I am writing to you.

Respectfully awaiting your reply,

Okapi

Subject: your complaint
Registration number: OK001
Status: Complete

Dear Okapi,

We read your
complaint with great interest.
We take every complaint very seriously,
and it is our duty to process each of them fairly.
Unfortunately, this book is only for
the *artiodactyla*.
Not for
the *perissodactyla*.

We would like to assure you
that we make no distinction
on the grounds of scent or color,
type of fur,
horns or antlers,
residence on steppe, rocks, or sand—
but we do count the number of toes.

We trust you will find our response satisfactory.

Respectfully yours,

The Editors

Feedback about your complaint

We would like to know if you were satisfied with how your complaint (registration number OK001) was handled.

Click one of the answers below:

Yes, I am satisfied.

Yes, I am very satisfied.

Don't know.

The Gerenuk

Here's what we would like to know:
Did you fly here in a UFO?
Non-stop, go, go, go,
all the way from
SciFi Land?
Do all the creatures
who live there have
eyes like that?
Ears like that?
Legs like that,
as thin
as wires?
Is your head full of
spiral galaxies,
dark matter,
solar winds?
Is that why you stand there
so perfectly still?

Beep beep,
can you hear us,
alien
from the multiverse?
Tell us:
what does a gerenuk
hope to find
on a planet
full of humankind?
Why did you come here?
When did you land?

Oh, so you've been here a while, have you?

The gerenuk
doesn't come from
Galactica,
but has lived
for millennia
in East Africa.
They never drink water,
and stand on their back legs
to eat leaves
from the highest branches.
They don't flee from danger,
but stand so still,
frozen, chilled,
like an alien statue,
on the spot.
In Somalia,
the name means:
giraffe-necked.

Ah, is that right?
Okay then,
creature from inner space,
please excuse us! Please defrost!
You're from here,
but we thought you were lost!
And it's because we'd never seen you too,
as so few zookeepers keep you in a zoo.
Too peculiar.
Too mysterious.
Too unfathomable.

So, little gerenuk
don't you worry,
there's no need for you to scurry.
We'll just leave you there to
chill!

The Pyrenean Ibex

It is with great sorrow
that the rangers of
Ordesa y Monte Perdido National Park
announce the passing of

CELIA
b. 1997 – d. January 6, 2000

As a result of a tragic accident—
a tree fell down and crushed her head—
the last Pyrenean ibex,
the *Capra pyrenaica*, is now dead.

There are no next of kin,
no family to miss her.
The last of her kind,
with no mate to kiss her.
Celia had never even dated.
Natural disasters,
not enough food,
exterminated.

Let's have a moment of silence,
let's ring the bells of mourning,
let's commemorate our sad loss.

Celia loved grass, herbs, and moss.

The Japanese Serow, or Kamoshika

Toyota,
sushi, samurai,
karate, Sudoku, Zen,
judo, ninja, Mazda,
origami, Mikado,
kamoshika—
wait a moment!

We speak quite a few words of Japanese.
We eat it,
we play it,
we drive it,
we know it,
but we don't know it all, do we?
Kamoshika?
Who or what is that?
Well?

Kamoshika is a goat
in wolf's clothing.
Living a secluded life in the forests,
sleeping between rocks,
balancing above ravines,
and . . .
. . . tasting so very, very good.
The serow was such a popular dish
that this animal almost disappeared from Japan.
So someone had to come up with a plan.
And indeed:
someone did!

This someone said:
"Let's shoot the serow!"
(This was in 1955,
when the war was not that long ago.)
"Let's shoot it right to the very top!"
"Huh?" said everyone.
"We'll make it a national monument!"
"Are you crazy?" everyone replied. "Is this a joke?"
No, it was perfectly serious—and sensible too,
because no one ever takes a bite out of national monuments.
And so the people let the serow be wild and free.

Result number 1:
Japanese people had to buy sushi more often instead.

Result number 2:
Too many serows all over the place,
even in people's backyards.

Kamoshika tsunami.
Emoji!
Haha!

The Moose

On a morning without light,
when the day has slipped away,
a tree comes to life,
branches lifting up,
trunk creaking with cold.
Breath billowing around its bark,
as it stretches to the sky.
Then it pulls its roots from the ground,
steps into the snow,
leaving an empty space
in that vast and chilly place.

Shuddering and shivering,
the tree shakes its top,
sways its branches.
Where is the morning?
Where is the sun?
Where is the grass, the moss, the bushes?
And where are the others?
Did they freeze on the first night of winter?

Oh, but wait . . .
. . . that steaming shadow wading the white fields,
it's not a tree. It's a male moose!
The largest deer in the world.
What's that on his head?
Looks like a stack of wood
big enough to heat the house all winter.
No, that bush of branches is his antlers,
which he flaunts to flirt with the females.

In the spring,
the male moose
takes up his weapons—
gradually,
sprouting steadily,
from the top of his head,
his antlers
grow up to an inch a day.
The older the male,
the bigger they grow,
so if a teen moose
bothers a female
when fall comes,
Grandpa waves his branches around
to say: Hey, you! Scram!

In the winter, when the snow covers the land,
the moose lays down his weapons,
and stops looking like a tree,
or a stack of wood,
and turns into a deer
strolling silently
through his neighborhood.

The Tapir

Hi everyone! I'm the tapir,
and I'm giving my presentation today about even-toed ungulates.

Even-toed ungulates can be found all over the world, except for Australia and Antarctica.
They're called that because their feet have an even number of toes—two or four.
I'm a tapir, so I have an odd number of toes: three, just like my mom and dad.
We belong to a small family. There are only fifteen species of odd-toed ungulates,
with one or three toes.
Rhinoceroses, zebras, donkeys, horses, and ponies—and that's it.
And if the northern white rhino dies out, our family will be even smaller.
There are over two hundred species of even-toed ungulates.
The lesser mouse-deer is the smallest, the hippopotamus is the biggest,
and the giraffe is the tallest.
Most even-toed ungulates have horns or antlers.
They eat plants, and they ruminate.
That means they chew their partially digested food over and over again.
Their scientific name is: *artiodactyla*.
Even-toed ungulates are more successful than odd-toed ones.
Sometimes I'd like to be even-toed,
but I'd have to lose a toe off each foot.
And I don't like the thought of that.
Anyway, sometimes it's good to be odd.
And my mom and dad tell me to stop complaining.
And that they love me as I am.
And maybe one day there'll be a book about us!
A book without any rhymes at all.
So that was my presentation.
Are there any questions?

P.S. If there are ever elections for even-toed ungulates, then I'll vote for the okapi!
P.P.S. Look! I made a rhyme—just one time!
P.P.P.S. And now I'm in this book too. Yay!

The Daeodon

When the earth still belonged to the earth,
and the sky, and the hills, and the water, and the wind,
when the earth was completely wild
and had never seen a goat,
a cow, a sheep,
when time
had no hands
and days had no name,
a beast roamed the world
that would make your hair stand on end.
It was a prehistoric giant,
the daeodon,
which means "hostile tooth."
Really, that's the honest truth.

The daeodon was an even-toed ungulate and an omnivore,
eating everything:
plants, bushes, trees, dead animals,
soil, stones, moon rocks, rubble.
Whatever its mouth could munch disappeared inside:
bones, marrow, bark and skin,
fur and tails, flesh and fin.
Terrorizing the vast plains
right from the very beginning,
daeodon, hell pig,
daeodon, trash can,
never losing, always winning.

When the earth still belonged to the earth,
to the rivers, the oceans, the volcanoes, the ice,
when the earth turned its turns without a worry,
wild and free and in no hurry,
the daeodon was not just a fossil,
not just a skeleton
rebuilt in a display case.

I wish the daeodon were alive today,
I'd invite it over to dine,
with drooling mouth and pounding feet,
with snapping teeth and swishing tail.
I'd tell it to leave the table alone,
and to eat the pan of kale.

The European Bison

You are:
the biggest land animal in Europe.
You are:
the grandchild of the steppe bison,
who once lived with the giant deer and the mammoth.
You are:
a gift once given to tsars and kings
in exchange for peace and other things.
You are:
a rare big grazer.
Nowadays you live fenced in,
in your barbed-wire home.
But in this book,
we'll give you a gift:
some space for you to roam,
in words and thoughts and a picture too,
and two whole pages, just for you.
Not like your grandmas and grandpas,
who once used to schlep
across the wide and endless steppe.

The Blue Wildebeest and the Giraffe Again

You are watching a live sports broadcast from Serengeti TV.
And now we're switching to our reporter on the spot,
Giraffa Tippelskirchi.
What's the mood like out there, G.T.?

Well, I can tell you that there's some tension.
I've been on the lookout for a few hours,
on the banks of the Mara River in Tanzania,
and just now on the horizon I saw
the first few clouds of dust appearing,
which means the blue wildebeests are on the way.
This is the big moment, viewers,
the one we've all been waiting for.
The moment of the annual crossing!
Yes, they're coming,
the blue wildebeests—the brindled gnus—
on the journey of a lifetime.
It's the survival of the fittest.
I can already see the vultures circling,
and the crocodiles are lined up and ready to go.

Thanks, G.T.! We'll be right back to you.
But first, a few words from our sponsors.

Are you bugged by parasites?
Now, from the company that brought you
the red-billed oxpecker,
we're introducing the . . . yellow-billed oxpecker!
Look for the orange discount sticker.
Three ticks a minute.

And it's back to you, G.T.!
What's the state of play?

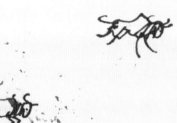

Well, as expected, it's pretty exciting.
The first wildebeest just got here,
followed by a line that's got to be ten miles long.
I can't see the end of it,
even though it's such a glorious sunny day,
and . . . if I'm not mistaken,
there's a pride of lions coming closer.
Who's going to survive out there?
Who's going to make it through today?
That's the big question.
No one's given the starting signal yet.
They're all looking at each other . . .
Number one has dropped back a few places.
The current in that river is pretty strong.
I can see the first few calves appearing now.

If you've just tuned in,
it's all about to begin.
That looks like an attempt—but no, it's a refusal!
Or just a practice run, who can say?

G.T., I'm sorry, but we're going to have to interrupt you again.

Want to enjoy the rainy season without any worries?
Then why not get an extra pair of eyes?
Bring along a zebra!
Zebras have excellent eyesight.
So grazing can be fun again!
Don't forget to check the unique barcode.

G.T., we're all ears!
What's been happening out there?

The moment of truth has arrived.
They're shoving and snorting,
the crocodiles are lurking under the water,
and yes, yes, here we go,
the first one's off,
jumping into the river.
What a daredevil, what courage,
and, oh, there go the rest of them,
And they're off, viewers!
They. Are. Off!
The water is churning.
I've lost count,
they're steaming and stamping.
I have a long neck (that's my superpower),
and believe me, it's chaos out there,
the crocodiles are on collision course,
and, oh oh oh, there goes the first wildebeest—under the
water . . .

Time for our sponsors, G.T.
Catch you later!

We all have days when we're sick of the numbers two and four.
When two's too much and four's a bore!
There's a simple solution—try one or three!
Choose something different! Be wild and free!
Hey, why be even when you could be odd?
Don't forget to consult your physician first!

Yes, G.T., go on, you're on screen.

Our first wildebeest has gone down,
and there goes number two, a calf.
There's no stopping it now!
They're dying out there!

This is costing lives—and points—
but the wildebeests have no choice,
the rain's on the other side of the river,
and the grass is greener over there.
One big bull is a horn's length in the lead,
but is he going to make it?
Yeeesss, yeeesss,
he's putting his hooves on the shore,
he's pulling himself up on the bank.
We have a winner, viewers,
and the rest are pouring after him.
Wet bodies, muddy bodies.
What a sensation out here on the savannah!
And aww, on the right of the picture,
you can see a little calf finding Mom again.
And with that heart-warming shot, we'll head back to the studio,
where *The Real Mousewives of the Mafinga Hills* is about to begin.

More about These Unusual Ungulates

(**Note:** all conservation statuses are drawn from the IUCN Red List of Threatened Species)

Giraffe

Giraffa camelopardalis

Region: Southern and Eastern Africa

Conservation Status: Vulnerable

A giraffe's head is over six feet away from its heart—that's a long way for blood to travel! Over 15 gallons of blood circulate around a giraffe's body every minute, pumped by the biggest heart of any land mammal. This strong heart isn't giraffes' only superpower: if you want to catch one napping, you'll have to be very lucky. A giraffe needs only 5 to 15 minutes of sleep every 24-hour period.

Bongo

Tragelaphus eurycerus

Region: Western and Central Africa (Lowland bongo); Eastern Africa (Mountain bongo)

Conservation Status: Near Threatened

Though bongos spend their days eating plants, they need salt to keep their coats a bright, glossy chestnut color. At night the animals head to mineral licks, where they can lap salt and other nutrients straight from the ground. If reaching a lick is too difficult, some bongos will even eat burnt wood and lightning-struck trees to get their salt for the day.

Wild Boar

Sus scrofa

Region: Eurasia and Northern Africa (introduced elsewhere)

Conservation Status: Least Concern

Scientists often call wild boars "opportunistic omnivores," since they'll eat almost anything they meet—fruits, nuts, eggs, and even small animals. Their long, narrow snout helps them root for food, and long, curved tusks help them fight with other pigs. Wild boars were probably domesticated at two separate times: once in China, and once in modern Turkey. Today's domestic pigs are their descendants.

Pig

Sus scrofa domesticus

Region: Worldwide

Conservation Status: Domesticated

Pigs don't wallow in mud because they're filthy slobs: they just want to cool down. Since pigs' sweat glands don't work very well, mud baths help them lower their body temperatures for longer than a swim in cold water. Some wild pigs also use dry, cracked mud to remove ticks, lice, and other parasites—so a roll in the mud might just be the best way to get clean.

Cape Buffalo (African Buffalo)

Syncerus caffer

Region: Sub-Saharan Africa

Conservation Status: Near Threatened

Weighing around a thousand pounds, the Cape buffalo is a massive, dangerous tank of an animal. They will start fights with lions, and they remember those who have harmed them for years. Still, Cape buffalo do have their tender moments. African buffalo herds lie touching each other, and—when one herd member is attacked—the others will rush to defend it.

Mountain Goat

Oreamnos americanus

Region: North America

Conservation Status: Least Concern

Mountain goats aren't actually goats at all! They're members of the antelope family, more closely related to deer than the domestic goat. Up high in places like the Rockies, mountain goats are often the largest mammals. These nimble creatures start climbing early: most mountain goats start exploring rocks with their mother only about a day after birth.

The Lesser Mouse-Deer (Lesser Malay Chevrotain)

Tragulus kanchil

Region: Southeast Asia

Conservation Status: Least Concern

The rabbit-sized lesser mouse-deer is tiny but mighty. Traditional Malaysian and Indonesian stories star Sang Kancil, a trickster mouse-deer who outwits creatures much larger than himself. But clever chevrotains aren't just for fables. When predators approach, male mouse-deer beat out a "drum roll" with their hooves (up to seven stomps per second). Terrified by the loud noise, many predators will run away from this tiny threat!

Common Warthog

Phacochoerus africanus

Region: Sub-Saharan Africa

Conservation Status: Least Concern

What we call warts, the warthog calls armor. The big, ugly bumps on its skin are actually thick, protective growths of skin. But cheetahs, lions, and hyenas don't care what warthogs look like: all they see is lunch! To escape these hungry predators, warthogs use their long legs to run up to 34 miles per hour.

Dik-Dik

Madoqua piacentinii, Madoqua kirkii, Madoqua saltiana, Madoqua guentheri

Region: Eastern and Southern Africa

Conservation Status: Least Concern

Named for their "squeaky toy" alarm call, dik-diks are minuscule antelopes that never grow beyond 16 inches in height. They mate for life, living in pairs instead of herds. But when their children reach seven months old, Mom and Dad will tell them to move out—Mom's probably already expecting another set of babies! It's time to find new territory and a mate.

Hippopotamus

Hippopotamus amphibius

Region: Eastern Africa, with scattered populations elsewhere

Conservation Status: Vulnerable

The hippopotamus's name comes from the ancient Greek for "river horse," and hippos certainly love spending time in the water. To cool down in the hot African sun, they splash into rivers and lakes, where they can hold their breath underwater for up to five minutes. Hippos also sweat an oily, red liquid that acts as both sunblock and bug repellent—who wouldn't want that in the summer?

Arabian Oryx

Oryx leucoryx

Region: Arabian Peninsula

Conservation Status: Vulnerable

The Arabian oryx is an amazing conservation success story: it was the first animal to be listed as "vulnerable" after previously being listed as "extinct in the wild" on the IUCN Red List. That's a three-rank jump! In the 1960s, only a few captive Arabian oryxes remained. But after decades of breeding in zoos, small herds of wild oryxes returned to Oman, Jordan, and the United Arab Emirates. Every year more oryxes are born, and the Arabian oryx moves further and further away from extinction.

Siberian Musk Deer

Moschus moschiferus

Region: Northern Eurasia

Conservation Status: Vulnerable

With its long, sharp fangs, you might mistake a Siberian musk deer for a vampire. But this animal is shy and timid, much happier nibbling plants than sucking blood. Male musk deer attract females with their gland pods, which produce a strong, earthy smell. Unfortunately, humans love the scent too—and they have hunted the deer for its musk gland for centuries. The Siberian musk deer and its musk deer cousins are all listed as vulnerable or endangered. Today most commercial musk scents are created synthetically, and captive breeding and habitat protection efforts are helping the deer survive into the next century.

Vicuña *(pronounced vi-KOON-ya)*
Vicugna vicugna

Region: Andes Mountains of South America

Conservation Status: Least Concern

Only a few decades ago, the national animal of Peru could have disappeared into extinction. The vicuña, a relative of the llama and alpaca, was hunted for its meat and softer-than-cashmere wool. Only 10,000 vicuñas remained by the 1960s. But now the vicuña is doing better than ever! Years of conservation efforts have helped increase their numbers and create more sustainable shearing practices. Today over 350,000 vicuñas rock their coats on their favorite high-altitude fashion runway: the Andes Mountains.

Wild Bactrian Camel
Camelus ferus

Region: Northern China and southern Mongolia

Conservation Status: Critically Endangered

Wild Bactrian camels called a nuclear test site home—and survived. China's Lop Nur region, home to some of the last Bactrian camels, was used to test nuclear weapons for more than forty years. But the animals continued to breed normally, and none of them appear to have been hurt by the radiation! Still, these camels face ongoing threats from hunters and mining operations. Only about 1,000 wild Bactrian camels remain, making this the eighth most endangered species on the planet. Scientists and conservationists continue to research new ways to protect this at-risk creature and its habitat.

White-Tailed Deer
Odocoileus virginianus

Region: Southern Canada to South America

Conservation Status: Least Concern

All fawns have spring or summer birthdays: baby white-tailed deer are born between April and July each year. Every fawn has white spots on its coat, but—like a human fingerprint—every fawn's pattern of spots is unique. When its mother goes to search for food, the spots help it hide from predators. But as the deer grows up, these spots will fade, and around its first birthday a male deer will grow its first set of antlers.

Okapi

Okapia johnstoni

Region: Central Africa

Conservation Status: Endangered

Nicknamed the "African unicorn," the okapi was unknown to science until the twentieth century. This striped relative of the giraffe has a long, agile tongue, perfect for plucking buds, leaves, and branches off tall trees. The tongue also makes a great washcloth: the okapi can lick its own ears and eyelids clean.

Gerenuk *(pronounced GARE-uh-nook)*

Litocranius walleri

Region: Horn of Africa

Conservation Status: Near Threatened

Though gerenuk means "giraffe-necked" in Somali, the gerenuk isn't the giraffe's fellow long-necked cousin. It's actually a member of the antelope family! The gerenuk holds two records in its family: longest-necked (of course) and highest unsupported reach. Balancing on its hind legs, without leaning against anything, the gerenuk can eat foliage up to 6 feet high.

Pyrenean Ibex

Capra pyrenaica pyrenaica

Region: Pyrenees Mountains of Europe

Conservation Status: Extinct

When Celia, the last known Pyrenean ibex, died in 2000, some of her cells survived. Frozen in liquid nitrogen, the cells helped scientists attempt a "de-extinction": resurrecting an extinct species through cloning. On July 30, 2003, a clone of Celia was finally born. But the animal unfortunately died a few minutes later, and the Pyrenean ibex is now the only animal to have ever gone extinct two separate times. Still, researchers hope that Celia's cells might one day return these beautiful, vanished creatures back to the Pyrenees.

Japanese Serow (Kamoshika)

Capricornis crispus

Region: Japan

Conservation Status: Least Concern

Though kamoshika were once hunted to near extinction, their numbers have grown and grown ever since gaining "national treasure" status in 1955. Today over 100,000 kamoshika live in the Japanese Alps and other forested areas. They've also flourished in Japanese culture—Yamaha sells a speedy Serow motorcycle, and Pokémon games include a kamoshika-inspired character. Hoping for the kamoshika's sure-footed certainty on their exams, nervous students might even buy a hoofprint-stamped charm.

Moose

Alces alces

Region: Northern regions of North America and Eurasia

Conservation Status: Least Concern

The largest of the deer species, moose are called elk in Europe. The name "moose" comes from the word *moosh*, meaning "bark-stripper," in the language of the Innu peoples of Quebec, Canada. A male moose's antlers are usually about 5 feet long, and Alaskan moose—the largest subspecies—can have even longer antlers, about 6 feet long. These big, brave creatures can defend themselves against a variety of predators, including cougars, grizzly bears, and wolf packs.

Tapir *(pronounced TAY-per)*
Tapirus indicus, Tapirus pinchaque, Tapirus terrestris

Region: South and Central America; Southeast Asia

Conservation Status: Endangered (Malay, Mountain); Vulnerable (Lowland)

Though related to horses and rhinos, the tapir looks like a cross between a pig and an anteater. Its long, flexible snout (similar to an elephant's trunk) is the perfect tool for sniffing out food, grabbing tasty plants, and even taking a dip. Tapirs don't really swim—instead, they walk along the bottom of rivers and lakes. When their heads are underwater, their snouts make excellent snorkels!

Daeodon *(pronounced DAY-oh-don)*
Daeodon shoshonensis

Region: North America

Conservation Status: Extinct

The daeodon, an enormous piglike mammal, lived in North America during the Miocene Age (about 29 million to 19 million years ago). Sometimes bigger than a bison, it was a member of the Entelodont family, which many people just call "killer pigs" or "hell pigs." Daeodons had sharp canine teeth and an appetite for fighting: paleontologists have found entelodont wounds on prehistoric camels and rhinos, as well as fellow entelodonts. Even the saber-toothed cat—which also roamed North America around that time—might have thought twice before attacking a killer pig.

European Bison (Wisent) *(pronounced VEE-ZENT)*
Bison bonasus

Region: Northeastern Asia

Conservation Status: Vulnerable

Famously depicted in cave paintings, bison have roamed Europe for centuries. But by the 1920s, only nine animals remained. Many worried that the North American bison's European cousin would go extinct. In 1938 the first European Bison Pedigree Book was published, detailing the genealogy of all surviving wisents. This system became the model for tracking other endangered species, and today several thousand European bison have returned to the wilds of their prehistoric ancestors.

Blue Wildebeest (Gnu)

Connochaetes taurinus

Region: Southern Africa
Conservation Status: Least Concern

Every year, wildebeests compete in the "World Cup of Wildlife." Each spring, they migrate between the Serengeti in Tanzania and the Maasai Mara in Kenya. Over a million wildebeests travel in search of new grazing grounds, joined by thousands of zebras, elands, and birds. But all this movement attracts predators. Lions, leopards, and hyenas watch for weak prey to attack; crocodiles snap and bite as the herds cross the Mara River. The dangerous trip finally ends in southwestern Kenya, where the wildebeests can rest in lush, green grazing pastures. Around October, the herds will return to the Serengeti, and the cycle will begin again.

For Further Reading and Discovery

Books

Montgomery, Sy, Roger Wood, and Logan Wood. *The Magnificent Migration: On Safari with Africa's Last Great Herds.* **Boston: Houghton Mifflin Harcourt, 2019.**

Acclaimed nature writer Sy Montgomery travels to the Serengeti to witness the wildebeests' annual migration to the Maasai Mara. Enhanced with full-color photos, the book explores the migration's impact on the environment and on other species.

Montgomery, Sy, and Nic Bishop. *The Tapir Scientist: Saving South America's Largest Mammal.* **Boston: Houghton Mifflin Harcourt, 2013.**

Sy Montgomery and photographer Nic Bishop join Brazilian biologists in their field work, adventuring into the Pantanal wetlands to gather information on the elusive tapir.

Raycroft, Mark. *Moose: Crowned Giant of the Northern Wilderness.* **Ontario: Firefly Books, 2017.**

Wilderness photographer Mark Raycroft describes the moose's habitats, antler cycle, and future in an increasingly warm climate.

Sartore, Joel. *Vanishing: The World's Most Vulnerable Animals.* **Washington, D.C.: National Geographic, 2019.**

Stunning, full-color photographs bring readers face-to-face with species on the brink of extinction, including ungulates like the critically endangered Sumatran rhinoceros.

Websites

Encyclopaedia Britannica. Various articles. britannica.com

The renowned encyclopedia features short, well-researched articles on the hooved creatures in this book, as well as photos, videos, and other media. Free access to the database is available through many public and academic libraries.

Giraffe Conservation Foundation. giraffeconservation.org

A family of organizations working to save giraffes in the wild, the Giraffe Conservation Foundation sponsors scientific research, breeding programs, and other initiatives in fifteen African countries. Their website spotlights current conservation efforts like Twiga Tracker, which uses GPS units to follow giraffes in their home ranges.

The International Union for Conservation of Nature (IUCN) Red List of Threatened Species. iucnredlist.org

The International Union for Conservation of Nature works to maintain biodiversity in animal, plant, and fungus species across the world. Since 1964, the IUCN has organized each organism on a scale from least to most danger of extinction: Least Concern, Near Threatened, Vulnerable, Endangered, Critically Endangered, Extinct in the Wild, and Extinct.

National Geographic Photo Ark. Animal Pictures and Facts. nationalgeographic.com/projects/photo-ark/explore

Featuring high-quality photos by Joel Sartore, these profiles describe multiple ungulates, including moose, African buffalo, and white-tailed deer. A short summary at the beginning of each page lists the animal's height, group name, average life span in the wild, and other interesting statistics.

Wild Camel Protection Foundation. wildcamels.com

Working with nature reserves and breeding programs, the Wild Camel Protection Foundation focuses exclusively on the Wild Bactrian Camel and its habitat. The foundation's website posts updates on current scientific research, conservation efforts, and breeding programs.

World Book Kids. Various articles. worldbookonline.com/kids/home

This children's encyclopedia presents reliable information about animals—including many of these ungulates—in a friendly, easy-to-read format. Access to the database is available through many public and academic libraries.